Ham

H KLICZKOWSKI

Ham

Dedicated to my friend Gabriel Neustadt, doctor
H. A. K.

H KLICZKOWSKI

Editor: **Paco Asensio**

Original Text: **Cristina Montes**

Translator: **David Hall**

Photographers: **Francesc Guillamet**
                     Roger Casas (pages 9 to 17)

Art Director: **Mireia Casanovas Soley**

Graphic Designer: **Emma Termes Parera**

Layout Pilar Cano

Copyright for the international edition:
© H Kliczkowski-Onlybook, S.L.
La Fundición, 15. Polígono Industrial Santa Ana
28529 Rivas-Vaciamadrid. Madrid
Tel.: +34 91 666 50 01
Fax: +34 91 301 26 83
asppan@asppan.com
www.onlybook.com

ISBN: 84-89439-11-7
D.L.: 22.853-02

Editorial Project

LOFT Publications
Domènech, 7-9 2° 2ª
08012 Barcelona. España
Tel.: +34 932 183 099
Fax: +34 932 370 060
e-mail: loft@loftpublications.com
www.loftpublications.com

Printed by:
Gráficas Anman. Sabadell, España.

July 2002

Acknowledgements
Iván Llanza, public relations of Sánchez Romero Carvajal Jabugo
SA; José Sánchez, of the Mesón 5 Jotas of Jabugo; Ferran Adrià,
of the Restaurante Bulli; Carme Ruscalleda, of the Restaurante
Sant Pau; Xavier Sagristà, of the Restaurante Mas Pau; Sergi Aro-
la, of the Restaurante La Broche.

Ham
Lifestyle

Ham Lifestyle

An intense aroma and breathtaking flavor... with credentials like these it is impossible not to succumb to the attractions of one of the most widely enjoyed and healthiest food products in existence.

Ham is one of the many gastronomical pleasures which originated among the common people, and though it has been recognized and enjoyed by kings and nobles, it has always maintained its tie to popular culture.

This is a product with deep roots in Spanish history and culture –and not just gastronomically speaking– which was born, like most truly basic things, out of a practical necessity, in this case the need to be able to keep food over longer periods of time. The lack of resources of those who set about to do this resulted in the ingenious solution of salting. According to popular wisdom, three spirits take part in curing ham, each one providing one of the three elements necessary for a matchless result –time, experience and imagination.

It is well known that the Mediterranean diet is one of the healthiest, richest and most varied in the world. The use of ham in many dishes in Mediterranean cuisine makes it a delicacy that is indispensable to anyone who wants to enjoy the many advantages of this cuisine.

Nonetheless, when one eats ham it is not just a treat for the palate. The nutritional values that it offers are many, and eating ham on a regular basis has important benefits for the organism. It helps the body to avoid certain diseases, since it is rich in B vitamins, particularly B1, B2 and niacin. It contains 50% more protein than fresh meat, and these proteins, in addition, assist tissue growth and renovation. It is a food product rich in iron, zinc,

magnesium, calcium and especially phosphorus, and its fat contains an important feature: the fatty acid is in large part oleic acid, typical of olive oil, which facilitates the production of so-called "good cholesterol" (HDL) while at the same time it helps to reduce the level of "bad cholesterol" (LDL).

More information. For everyone who is concerned about their figure, there is no need to worry. Ham contains very few kilocalories and is highly recommended for dieting.

Ham is, as can be seen, a real delight that everyone can enjoy, a tasty, succulent treat whose specific attributes make it possible for us to qualify it as a food product that is unique in the world, a product with a history and tradition that we are about to explore.

In this book the reader will discover myths and stories but will also learn where the best hams are produced, what process is used to create each piece, the different types of ham there are and their denominations of origin, and the best recommendations on how to cut and keep them fresh.

This work is thus a magnificent, useful guide to one of the most delicious, nutritious, appetizing and pleasurable foods in the world.

The Pig

The Pig

From ears to hooves, practically every part of the pig is put to some use. It can boast of being one of the animals that are of greatest benefit to humanity, but it has also inspired terrific controversy down through history. The pig has left no one indifferent. Many have paid tribute to the delights it has to offer, but it is no less true that it has also been an object of contempt since time immemorial.

In many places, the pig in ancient times was a sacred species, worshipped and believed to be the repository of a higher power. It was an animal under special protection, which could not be touched or sacrificed.

The Arameans considered it a totem animal; the Egyptian religion protected it and only allowed its meat to be eaten during the full moon, when it contributed to sanctifying of the spirit. Even for the Hebrews, who now do not eat it at all, eating its meat was a ritual of purification.

For most cultures the pig has symbolic connotations. In the Orient it is associated with life cycles and is a sign of good fortune. Its white color and curved form are the image of the waxing moon, symbol of life after death. In the Buddhist wheel of existence the pig represents ignorance, and in other civilizations it is associated with carnal desire.

The Celts used this animal in many of their religious ceremonies, while it was at the same time one of the staples of their diet. The ancient Greeks employed the profile of the head of a wild pig to represent the image of the hero, and the Romans considered its meat and by-products as delicacies.

The pig, evidently, has excellent references, but history has shown that it did not enjoy the approval of everyone. Hebrew lawmakers ended up prohibiting the eating of pork, and centuries later Mohammed, in setting down the principles of the Koran, extended the aversion

Though it is said that everything from the pig is put to some use, the most highly regarded part of its body are the back legs. From them, we get ham, one of the most highly prized treasures of the Mediterranean diet.

to this animal that originated with the Hebrews to all of Islam. An attitude that has lasted into our own time. Today, its use as food is forbidden to both Arabs and Jews.

Some anthropologists, such as Marvin Harris explain both cultures hostility to the pig using theories that are not based on religious beliefs. Harris affirms that this abomination was a response to needs of another sort and is convinced that they condemned the animal "because the pig was a menace to the natural and cultural ecosystems of the Middle East".

The Hebrews lived in arid regions and depended for their livelihood mainly on herds of sheep, goats and cows and on an agriculture based mainly on pasturelands. Thus the prohibition against eating pork was in fact an excellent ecological strategy. It would have been extremely difficult to adapt the pig to the geographic and climatic conditions of these areas. The pig is an animal accustomed to woods and river banks with abundant vegetation. It is omnivorous, though it cannot survive exclusively on grass. It eats fruit, tubers and grain, which puts it into direct competition with humans. Due to its physical characteristics it cannot be moved over long distances, and it is not a source of milk like goats and sheep —the first animals to be domesticated in the Middle East— or cattle, which also provide skins, fiber and meat. Raising pigs in these areas would have meant raising animals whose meat was a kind of luxury item.

To these natural disadvantages we must add the fact that between 7000 and 2000 B.C. the population of the region was multiplied more than fifty-fold, which led to irreversible consequences in the ecosystem. The pig was inescapably destined for exile. Religious leaders undertook to solve the problem by banning the eating of pork. Necessity made this a divine prohibition. This ancient dietary law is still in force today, and even in areas far from the Middle East, the vast majority of Jews and Muslims abstain from consuming the products derived from the pig.

On the other hand, the pig played an important role in the daily life of many other peoples, including those of the Iberian Peninsula. In Spain the pig has always had the approval of the greatest part of the population. Attesting to this are saints like San Antón, San Martín or Santa

The pig forms one of the spiritual borderlines between the three cultures that coexisted in Spain for centuries, Christians, Arabs and Jews, since it constitutes a fundamental difference in dietary customs.

Inmaculada who were patrons of the production of pork products, the fact that centuries ago specialists in the butchering of the animal enjoyed great social prestige and that the art of preparing pork products and salting and curing ham has survived down to our own day and has become one of the most important and respected aspects of our gastronomic heritage.

The pig is a domesticated mammal of the swine family which is extensively raised all over the world. It belongs to the class of animal with an even number of toes and to the sub-class of animals with 44 teeth. It is a quick, intelligent animal and its period of gestation is short (little more than a hundred days.). The adult pig has a heavy, rounded body, a long, flexible snout, short legs with cleft hooves and a short tail. Its skin, which can be of different colors, is thick, though not lacking in sensitivity, and is covered in some parts with coarse bristles.

Everything seems to indicate that the pig descends from two species of wild swine, one European and the other coming from southeast Asia. Fossils of wild pigs have been found in forests and swamps of Eurasia, which indicate that this animal is more than 40 million years old. It was domesticated in China about 4,900 years before the beginning of our era and in Europe around 1,500 B.C. Pigs were introduced into America by Columbus and subsequent Spanish expeditions that landed in the New World. It is believed that in the Middle Ages domestic pig populations were divided into three large groups: Asiatic pigs (descended from Sus Vitatus, breeds originating in China and Indochina), northern pigs (descended from Sus Scrofa, from central and northern Europe) and Mediterranean pigs (descended from Sus Mediterraneus, from the Mediterranean coast).

The domestication of the pig in Europe is considered to have taken place about 1,500 B.C., though fossils of wild pigs found in Eurasia indicate that the animal is more than 40 million years old.

Raising

Few animals enjoy a quality of life like the Iberian pig's. The special program for its care and feeding can only be compared with the treatment reserved for fighting bulls. The Iberian pig is raised in absolute freedom, allowing the animal to run and get the exercise that is vital for its particular way of storing fats and developing its muscles, and its diet is based on natural products. Its natural habitat and traditional area for feeding is the wooded pastureland known as the "dehesa" (term coming from Latin, which literally means "defense"), incomparable paradise of the Iberian pig consists of vast expanses of open land that are a perfect environment for raising this animal.

The "dehesa", without which it is impossible to comprehend the life of the Iberian pig, is essentially a natural park wooded with cork and holm oak. In Spain the "dehesa" extends over almost two and a half million hectares, located in the southeast of the country, in Western Andalusia, Salamanca, Extremadura and a strip of land running through the provinces of Segovia, Toledo, Ávila, Ciudad Real, Jaén and Granada.

These typical types of trees that fill the "dehesa" provide the animal with its basic food: the acorn, a nut that makes for a diet low in protein, fat and cellulose, but rich in carbohydrates, easily convertible into fats. It has a lot of calories, 50% of starches, sugar, some fat, abundant Vitamin C and carotene. During the fattening period, called "montanera", a pig can eat up to 22 pounds of acorns a day. On the basis of these trees a selective system of stock raising has evolved that is based on an absolute interdependence between the animal and the environment. This feeding in the wild, which the pig begins at the age of 10 to 14 months, is supplemented with grasses, wild fruits and nuts and small animals such as reptiles, insects and snails. In the end weight reaches between 175 and 250 pounds.

The "montanera" season covers a period of four or five months, from December to April, approximately, which corresponds, logically, with the months of the acorn season.

The authentic Iberian pig grows in the "dehesas". In these natural parks in western and southwestern Spain a unique breed of pig that constitutes a genuine genetic heirloom lives in freedom.

Classification

The names of the different types of pig reflect the main uses they are put to. At present there are about 90 recognized breeds and more than 200 varieties. It is believed that the first pigs arrived on the Iberian Peninsula with the Phoenicians and once here interbred with the indigenous wild boars which were abundant toward the end of the Mesolithic period, which explains the peculiarities of the Iberian breeds.

Up to the beginning of the 20th century there were two great indigenous pig populations in Spain, differing both in origin and habitat.

On the one hand, the **Iberian pigs** were in the west and southwest of the peninsula. Their natural habitat and diet differed greatly from those of the other population: vast stretches of Mediterranean forests with wooded meadows rich in holm and cork oak, whose fruit is the acorn. The Iberian branch includes the Interpelado from the Pedroches valley, the Chato Murciano, the Black Lampiño from Guadiana, the Black Canary pig and what are known as the red strains: Torbiscal, Campiñeso, Retinto and Manchado de Jabugo. The Iberian pig is an exceptional breed, unique of the species, which represents thousands of years of adaptation and centuries of patient selection and breeding aimed at producing a perfect animal. Over the years, its territory has been reduced to certain very specific geographical areas. In fact, its natural environment is limited to the eight Spanish provinces in the southwest corner of the country, along with Algarve and Alentejo, regions of Portugal on the border with Spain.

The distinguishing physical characteristics of the Iberian group are long, slim, strong legs, sharp snout, sparse, delicate hair and dark coloring of the skin and hooves. It should be mentioned that this dark color typical of some strains of the Iberian group has given rise to the nickname "pata negra" (black leg), which has gradually come to be used for Iberian hams in general; but it is important not to forget that there can be Iberian hams that are not "pata negra".

It is both arbitrary and simplistic to identify the Iberian pig with the black pig, since the group includes numerous subdivisions that can be classified in terms of functional characteristics, physical traits, color of skin, bristles, etc.

Its most important quality is a genetic peculiarity which makes it possible for it to store large deposits of lipids that infiltrate the muscle mass and create the characteristic white streaks that give the meat an incomparable texture, aroma and oiliness.

The other great group is **Celtic pigs**, a classification that includes the Galician, the Chato Victoriano, the Baztán from Navarra and the Lermeño of Burgos, all of them in the northeast part of the country, were to be found in Atlantic type forests and areas with a mild climate. In time this group has led to what is know as the white pig, result of cross-breeding between strains like the Landrade, Duroc, Large White or Belgian White, among others. These animals are raised in stalls and fed on cereal-based natural fodders. They do almost no exercise and they are raised under supervision until they are slaughtered, when they are five to six months old and have reached a weight of about 200 pounds.

These pigs are the ones that provide the "serrano" hams, whose quality is determined by the castration of the pigs, their weight and total fat content. The curing process for "serrano" hams is identical to the process for Iberian hams, with some difference in the drying time. In spite of the differences between Iberian and "serrano" hams, in terms of geographical locations, breeds of pig, and flavor and aroma, this variety of ham is also a product of great culinary value and has excellent nutritional value.

On the other hand, if we compare Iberian ham with other European cured hams, a number of differences appear. In the Italian Parma and San Daniele hams, for example, there is a lower moisture content in the final product, giving a firmer texture and more intense flavor. French ham has a different taste and is sold without the hoof and with the skin of the tip cut off. The German Speck is smoked.

The peculiarities of the Celtic pigs caused them to be used principally in the production and marketing of pork products and fresh meat. The Iberian pig, on the other hand, is used for preparation of products cured over long periods of time

Iberian Ham Categories

There are three categories of Iberian ham established on the basis of the type of nourishment. Iberian acorn-fed ham comes from pigs that have lived in conditions of semi-freedom during the last four months of their lives and have fed basically on acorns, from which they assimilate oils. This means that 50% of their initial weight is gained with these nuts. The second category corresponds to the "recebo" or half-acorn Iberian ham, coming from pigs that, beginning the "montanera" period with a weight of between 185 and 250 pounds, supplement their weight (the maximum required for the three categories may not exceed 395 pounds) by feeding on acorns and finish the fattening period with authorized fodder. The third category is the fodder pigs, with this product providing more than 30% of their weight.

The attention devoted to the care of the animal from birth, as well as its feeding, are of capital importance and have a decisive influence on the quality of its meat. Factors such as the purity of the breed, the type of feeding and the curing system employed condition the final quality of the Iberian hams.

The holm oak is the Iberian tree par excellence and has always played an important role in the economy of the people of the Mediterranean. One of the most important benefits it provides is the acorn, the favorite food of the Iberian pig.

The Industry

The Industry

The habitat of the Iberian pig extends over thirteen Spanish provinces, though only eight of them are involved in the industrial transformation of their products, work which is undertaken by companies that are located more than 1,640 feet above sea level. The most important are to be found in Jabugo, Cortejana and Cumbres Mayores in Huelva; Guijuelo, Ledrada and Candelario, in Salamanca; Piernal and Monández in Cáceres; Villanueva and Pozoblanco in the Los Pedroches valley in Córdoba; Hontoria and Cantimpalos in Segovia; Ronda and Benahoján in Málaga, and Jerez de los Caballeros, Zafra, Frenegal de la Sierra, Higuera la Real, Monesterio and Fuentes de León, in Badajoz.

The majority of these firms are small in size and handle the complete process (slaughter, quartering, cooling, dryer and storing), although at present industries are developing in which the slaughterhouse is separate from premises devoted to the subsequent processes.

There are no precise references, but it is estimated that industrial curing of products coming from the Iberian pig appeared towards the end of the 19th century and that the mule drivers of Salamanca were pioneers in this activity. It appears that the first industries were set up in Guijuelo and in Candelario, and from there the activity spread toward the south until it reached the mountain ranges of Andalusia.

At present there are three great industrial areas: Salamanca, a province which hosts more than a hundred industries, with its most important center in Guijuelo; Extremadura, with more than thirty factories engaged in this work between Cáceres and Badajoz; and Huelva, with a large number of companies registered in important points such as Jabugo, Cortejana and Cumbres Mayores.

The habitat of the Iberian pig ranges over thirteen provinces, but only eight of them have industrial plants devoted to processing its products.

1. Cumbres de Enmedio
2. Jabugo (Sánchez Romero Carvajal properties)
3. Alajar
4. Almonaster de la Sierra
5. Candelario
6. Ledrada
7. Zona Cortejana. Jabugo
8. Candelario
9. Fuentes de León
10. Linares de la Sierra
11. Jabugo
12. Cortejana
13. Jabugo

Curing process

One of the first written references containing a recipe for salting and curing ham appears in the book, "De Re Agricola", by Cato the Censor who died in 149 B.C. Other writings show that the Romans gave homage to the fine qualities of this product from the Emperor Diocletian to the historian Marco Verro, and including the poet Marcial, who praised the virtues of this delicacy in his "Epigrams". Works such as Strabo's "Geography", Apicius' cookbook or Book XII of the treatise "De Re Agricola" by Lucius Moderatus Columela serve as testimony to the high regard Mediterranean lands have always held for ham. A devotion that has come down to our own time and spread worldwide, gradually acquiring more enthusiasts. Helmut Kohl, Luciano Pavarotti and the Queen of England are some of the admirers of this succulent delicacy.

The process of salting and curing hams, like the preparation of other food products that is still done using traditional methods today, was born of the need to find a way to keep the meat from slaughtered animals in good condition over longer periods of time. Years, observation and experience have made the resulting process one of the major achievements of Spanish gastronomy.

Experience, time and imagination are, according to an old popular saying, the spirits that act together to give ham the flavor and aroma that make it an exquisite treat, though good raw material is essential as well.

Though it is not known precisely where people first conceived the present methods of salting, curing and ageing Iberian hams, a system which is virtually identical in all the different areas, the ham industry as we know it today has its origins in the traditional domestic slaughter that was practiced and is practiced even today in self-sufficient societies.

This is undoubtedly a question of a master recipe shaped down through the centuries and that has been perfected through its history by the patient and

To check the aroma, and thus the quality, of a piece, the expert ham-maker must proceed to the "cala". In other words, he inserts a horse or cow bone, prepared according to traditional methods, between the joints of the ham.

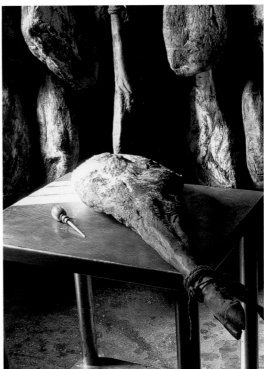
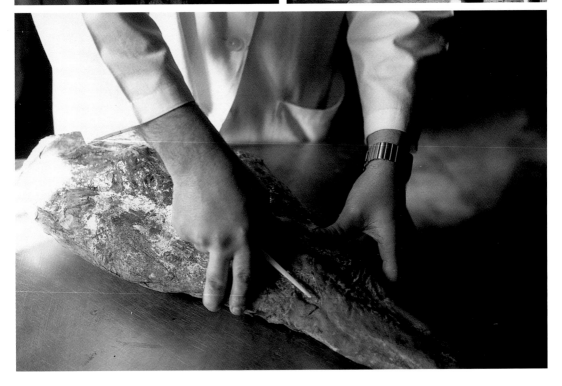

methodical observations of a craft system based on intuition and an ability to wait.

The first step in the process is in the slaughterhouse, where the pigs arrive after a journey that varies in length. Before being slaughtered the animal must be allowed to rest for a period of not less than twenty four hours so as to regulate the pH level in the meat and calm down after the trip.

Winter is the ideal time for slaughtering, since among the key factors in the curing process are the environmental changes that occur with this season of the year. Once the animal has been bled, it is cut up in the typical "serrano" way, and the skin is branded with the date of the slaughter. After the salting phase, the hams are put into the chilling area where a curing process begins that will bear fruit after between 18 and 24 months, when warm, summer temperatures have made their appearance.

Low temperatures and high humidity, factors that maintain an inversely proportional relation —less temperature, higher percentage of humidity— bring about a gradual, natural and spontaneous transformation of the original product.

The amount of salt must be exactly right to protect the piece from microbial alterations and obtain, at the same time, an appetizing flavor. During salting pieces are piled one on top of the other, up to a maximum of eight hams in the pile, and are separated from one another only by the layer of sea salt that covers them. They remain like this at a temperature of between 33 and 44 degrees for a period of one day per kilo of weight. This phase of the process is of tremendous importance, because a quality ham should not be salty but, on the contrary, should have a sweet taste.

The penetration of the salt into the inside of the ham produces a progressive dehydration. The industry applies the salt and establishes conditions adequate for making possible the transformation of certain substances of the ham (fats and proteins) through complex bio-chemical processes.

What transforms the piece into ham is a balance of the distribution of salt inside, outside temperature, fat, loss of humidity and time.

The salt is subsequently removed by washing the

One of the first phases of the curing process, identical in all types of ham, is salting. The pieces are stacked one on top of the other with cooking salt between them. The hams remain like this one day for each kilogram of weight, as may be observed here on the premises of the company Sánchez Romero Carvajal.

pieces, and they go into a settling or post-salting period. After this phase thay go are put into natural drying rooms, where they stay for six to nine months and where there takes places what is known as the "sudado" (literally, sweating) caused by the summer heat. The drying rooms are installed in the upper parts of the factories, and in domestic production in the attics or lofts of homes. The hams hang from the ceiling so that moisture is slowly eliminated. They lose most of the liquid and the fat is distributed among the muscle fibers. The physical and biochemical changes that occur modify both the appearance –the dripping of fat is increased when it coincides with the summertime– and the "aroma".

Afterward, the hams are moved again. They are taken down to the "bodegas" (cellars) to ensure a slow ageing process and conclude the final phase of curing and refining. In these, dimly lit, silent rooms, where temperature and humidity are maintained at fixed levels, the ham is kept for between ten and twelve months. It is in this environment that the fungi that tend to cover the surface of the ham develop. Under the action of the microflora, fat is stabilized, reaching the precise point of texture and juiciness that will mark the ham's "aroma".

On coming out of the "bodega", after having lost between 30-35% of its original weight, the next step is the "cala". In other words a bone from a cow or horse, prepared according to tradition methods, is inserted between the joints of the ham in order to check its aroma. When the bone, or "cala", is removed, the ham should give off a strong, pleasant smell that is proof of its quality.

As occurs with fine wines, there are a whole series of rituals centered around Iberian ham, which experts know perfectly. For the novice, a few key points can help to recognize a good "pata negra" (for the color of the skin). The choice of a good ham depends on its shape (like a violin), color (red), fat, salting, "aroma" and flavor.

During the drying phase, the pieces are hung up to eliminate moisture. They remain in this position for six to nine months, during which the ham îsweatsî and the fat is distributed among the fibers, creating its typical appearance, texture and color.

The Ham

The ham

Rumor has it that one of the best gifts the Spanish diplomatic corps can offer official visits is a good Iberian ham.

And if it is true that the hams that enjoy the greatest prestige in Spain are the hams from Jabugo, Extremadura and Cáceres, it should be kept in mind that there are many others and that, in addition, this is not the most correct way of designating them, since these terms refer solely to their geographical point of origin. One can find several types of ham in the same region, depending on the pig, his nutrition and the curation process that has been followed.

The typical "aromas", flavors and textures of ham are due, most of all, to its fat. The richness of its nutrients is very different from that of the meat it is made from.

Among pork products, ham is the one with the greatest number of denominations of origin or specific denominations. With these denominations both the authorities responsible and the producers seek to assure the quality of the product being offered and the quality of its processing. Ham has a total of five denominations of origin (DO), one specific denomination (DE) and one quality denomination (DC): Jamón de Teruel, Guijuelo, Dehesa de Extremadura, Jamón de Huelva, Los Pedroches, Jamón de Trévelez and Jamón Riojano.

In Spain, the Regulation Council is the agency in charge of dealing with everything related to the denominations. Its functions are, among others, to prepare and maintain the different registers; to advise, observe and supervise production, conditions and quality; to qualify the product and promote or defend the DO, DE and DCs. It is also responsible for approving the commercial labels of each of the registered firms.

In 1984, the first DO in Spain came into effect, **Jamón de Teruel**, third in the world in chronological order after the hams of San Daniele and Parma. The magnificent climatic conditions of the province make it possible to produce cured hams of excellent quality. The Morellan and Segovian pigs native to the area have been replaced by the Landrade, Landrade White and Duroc strains, and only them and their crossbreeds can be held under this DO. The minimum age for slaughtering these pigs is eight months. The period for salting the pieces is relatively short —one day in salt per kilogram of weight— and the minimum curing process lasts approximately one year. The physical characteristics of these pieces are a weight that is never less than seven kilos (15 pounds), an elongated, narrow shape rounded at the edges until the muscle appears, and the conservation of the outer surface and the hoof. Its color is bright red when cut and the fat is partially infiltrated into the muscle mass. This fat, which covers the bone, with its mild aroma and whitish yellow color, is oily in consistency and its flavor is sweet and pleasant.

The art of salting and curing hams is a gastronomical heritage that has survived and been perfected down through the centuries. Its preparation, which is simple and based on traditional methods, makes it a healthful, delicious product.

The DO **Guijuelo** began its activities in the year 1986, thus becoming the second DO created by the National Institute of Denominations of Origin in Spain and the fourth in Europe. Its production area is made up of the dehesas belonging to the autonomous communities of Castilla-León, Extremadura, Andalucía and Castilla-La Mancha, and the area where these products are processed comprises some 77 municipalities situated in the southeast part of the province of Salamanca. These are hams cooled by the icy winds and cold of an area that is more than three thousand feet above sea level. The history of making ham in the traditional way in this area go back to the 19th century, and undoubtedly it is this experience, together with the care and skill of the workers, that make for results that are more than admirable – sweet tasting hams that have been a short time in salt. Depending on the quality, this denomination distinguishes two classes of hams and paletas (shoulders). On the one hand the acorn-fed Iberian ham and paleta, coming from Iberian pigs that have eaten fodder, grass and stubble up to 200 pounds and completing the rest of their weight (350-420 lbs.) with acorns and grasses typical of the "dehesa" during the "montanera" season; and on the other hand, Iberian ham and paleta from Iberian pigs that have reached 90 lbs. eating fodder, grass and stubble and reaching their full weight with acorns, grasses typical of the "montanera" season, and fodder, or only fodder.

The DO **Dehesa de Extremadura** was created in 1990 with the objective of supervising and promoting the hams and paletas from areas devoted to raising pigs, composed of the dehesas located in the autonomous community of Extremadura, and the areas involved in processing, in the Extremadura counties of the mountains of the southwest of Badajoz, Ibor-Villuercas, Cáceres-Gredos Sur, Sierra de Montánchez and Sierra de San Pedro.

This denomination includes three classes of products: acorn-fed Iberian ham and paleta, coming from animals that feed exclusively on acorns and grasses during the montanera season; Recebo Iberian ham and paleta, from pigs fed on acorns and grasses together with a supplement of approved fodders; and Cebo Iberian ham and paleta, coming from pigs fed only on approved fodder.

Although the pig is a very common domesticated mammal all over Spain, there are specific areas, such as Andalusia, Extremadura or Castilla, which can claim to raise the very best ham.

Areas with denomination of origin

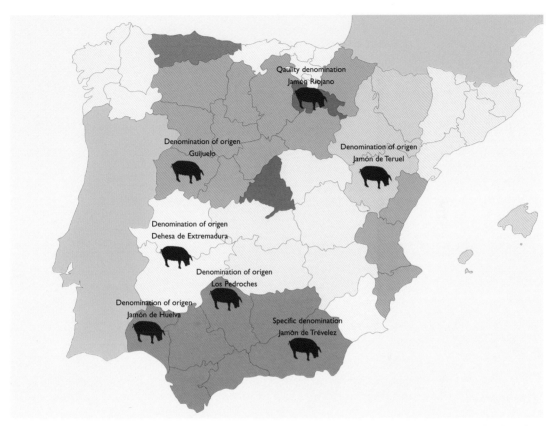

Qaulity denomination
Jamón Riojano

Denomination of origen
Guijuelo

Denomination of origen
Jamón de Teruel

Denomination of origen
Dehesa de Extremadura

Denomination of origen
Los Pedroches

Denomination of origen
Jamón de Huelva

Specific denomination
Jamón de Trévelez

Among all pork products, ham is the one that has accumulated the greatest number of denominations of origin, five in all, as well as specific and quality denominations. Products covered by one of these denominations must bear a label that guarantees their authenticity.

The particular mountainous character of the land, characterized by ample extensions of the Extremadura "dehesas", coupled with a continental climate with a moderate influence of the Atlantic and the patience, care and tradition that characterize the craftsworkers who prepare these pieces together succeed in obtaining a high-quality product with a legendary and unmistakable taste and aroma.

The DO **Jamón de Huelva** began its work of supervision and promotion of Iberian hams and paletas in the year 1995. Its production areas consist of the "dehesas" of Extremadura and Andalusia (provinces of Cáceres, Badajoz, Cádiz, Córdoba, Huelva, Málaga and Sevilla), where the fattening of Iberian pigs during the "montanera" period is traditional. Processing areas are limited to 31 municipalities in the national park of Sierra de Aracena y Picos de Aroche, of which Jabugo, Cortejana and Cumbres Mayores are the most famous.

The existence of "dehesas" devoted to the production of acorns for fattening pigs figures historically in the Charter of Montánchez, dated 1236. Lope de Vega also dedicated some of his verses to the ham produced in the Sierra de Aracena. There is, thus, a very long tradition in the area.

Within this denomination of origin, there are three distinct classes of products: acorn-fed, recebo, and fodder-fed Iberian hams and paletas, pieces that are typically elongated, slim and finely shaped by the typical "serrano" cut in V (for the paletas a "half moon" cut is also permissible, though in both cases the hoof is kept). Though Jabugo still does not have its own denomination of origin responsible for classifying the hams produced in this area, the hams from this Huelva locality are worthy of special mention as a point of reference. The name is a noble one in the world of ham, since these are pieces whose quality is taken for granted. The climatic conditions of the Huelva mountain range, along with the particular micro-flora that characterizes it are the two most important factors in the quality of these excellent hams.

Los Pedroches, a DO dating from 1998, has as its objectives to protect the Iberian pig products from its areas of production and processing, in various municipalities of the Province of Córdoba.

Each of the commercial labels used by the different registered firms must be approved by the Regulation Council, which is in charge of supervising the denominations of origin and issuing the seals and numbered back labels to be put on the product for commercial sale.

The Arabs christened this area Fahs al Ballut, which means the plain of the acorns. The name was later changed to the Los Pedroches valley, in reference to the decomposed granite that makes up the composition of its fertile soil and to the stones typically employed in its architecture.

It seems to be an historical fact that during the second half of the 19th century the limited production of ham coming from **Trévelez** was authenticated at point of origin by the city councilmen of this town of the Alpujarras. The reasons for its former prestige have practically disappeared, although pieces from Trévelez continue to be an unavoidable reference in the context of Spanish hams.

Rioja hams have obtained a denomination of quality. In this zone as well, the pig clearly constitutes one of the basic elements of the local cuisine, and the products obtained from it are of high quality.

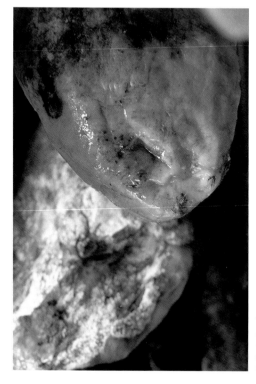

The technical services of the DO are in charge of supervising the raising of Iberian pigs to guarantee the quality of the hams and paletas that reach the ultimate consumer.

Parts of the Ham

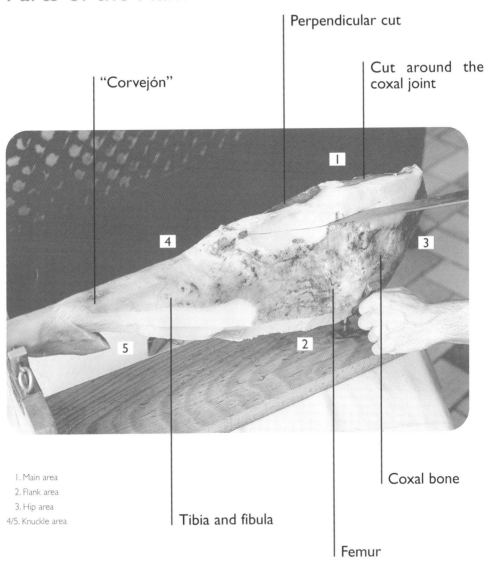

Perpendicular cut

Cut around the coxal joint

"Corvejón"

1

4

3

5

2

1. Main area
2. Flank area
3. Hip area
4/5. Knuckle area

Tibia and fibula

Coxal bone

Femur

Ham on the plate

Ham is a select, deluxe food item that should not be eaten straight from the "bodega". It is necessary to wait about two days for it to get acclimatized and reach an interior temperature of between 73° and 77° F. But it is not advisable for the ham to be too long in the stores that sell them or in the home before being eaten either, since changes in temperature, humidity and other factors can affect its taste.

In commercial establishments the hams should be hung in properly lighted and ventilated places with enough space between the pieces so that they do not touch.

No need for surprise if you find the ham covered with fat, since that is what protects the product and extends its shelf life. A layer of whitish mold often appears on the skin, indicating that the ham has spent time in the bodega; this is not injurious and can be eliminated by wiping it off with oil, using a clean moist cloth.

There are certain guidelines for cutting the ham which help to get the most from it. It is best to begin for the part that is most cured and continue into the softer areas, which are the ones that are covered with the most fat. If cut with a knife, hams will usually give a net output of about 50% the original weight.

Commercial establishments usually offer the ham without the bone, but it should still have the skin and fat. In these cases it is usual to keep it refrigerated, and when it is at room temperature it gives off a yellowish liquid. This is melted fat, and does not effect the ham's suitability for consumption, since it does not alter it in any way.

Once the piece has been started it should be kept at a temperature of between 35° and 50° F., avoiding contact with other products that give off strong smells and keeping the hams properly separated so that they can breathe and mold does not appear.

A ham has three clearly differentiated parts. The one that often has the greatest amount of fat content is the flank or "maza". This is a highly appreciated part and a gre-

The expert in charge of cutting the ham should use a long, thin, flexible, perfectly sharpened knife to obtain a correct cut.

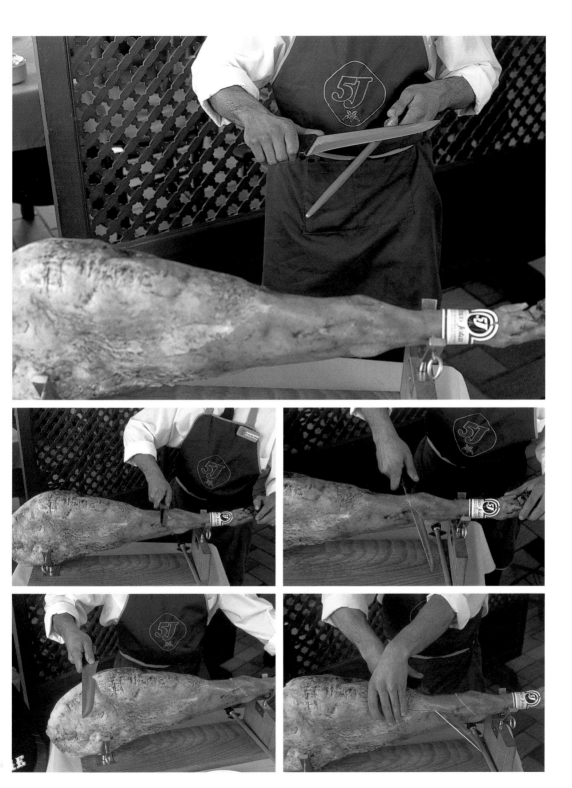

. Flavors and "aromas" change depending on the part of the ham. The first cut, which offers a considerable amount of fat content, is sweeter than the slices obtained as we get closer to the bone.

at deal of ham can be obtained from it. The inner flank, or "contramaza", on the opposite side offers much less meat. It is narrow, normally less cured and is firmer, with less fat both on the outside and in the meat itself. The part opposite the hoof and furthest from the center of the ham is called the tip. It tends to be very tasty, with a high fat content. However, if it is not adequately covered with fat it may come out a bit too salty. The part just below the hoof is what is called the hock and this is where the piece should be held.

If you want to appreciate the full "aroma" and taste of this exquisite delicacy, the ham should be served at room temperature; cold it loses its flavor almost entirely. It is not advisable to leave it in the refrigerator either. The best thing to do is to cut the amount you need right before serving.

To truly enjoy good ham it must be cut correctly. Tradition requires that it be cut by the hand of an expert. The cutting of Iberian ham by hand is a genuine ritual that calls for great skill and experience. From the first incision until the bone is left clean, each stage requires its own special touch with the knife. Slices should be thin, almost transparent, and should have a bit of fat on them.

Holding the ham with one hand is something that is reserved for genuine master specialists. The piece is supported on a cutting table while held with one hand. For those who do not have the good fortune to be experts, the best thing to do is to use a "jamonero", a special support designed to hold the piece firmly at both ends.

A knife to be used specifically to cut the ham is very sharp, with a long, narrow, flexible blade. To clean off the skin and fat, the knife should have a wide blade. Before proceeding to the art of cutting off fine, equal slices, the person cutting the ham should clean the piece, removing the skin and excess fat. The pieces of skin should be put to one side, in order to use them later to cover the part of the ham that is exposed when the cutting is done. When this phase is finished, with the hoof held up, cutting is begun at the narrowest part (the inner flank), which is the part that dries out most quickly because it has the least amount of fat. Slices are cut lengthwise from the hoof to the tip, and the cutting surfaces should

Flavors and "aromas" change depending on the part of the ham. The first cut, which offers a considerable amount of fat content, is sweeter than the slices obtained as we get closer to the bone.

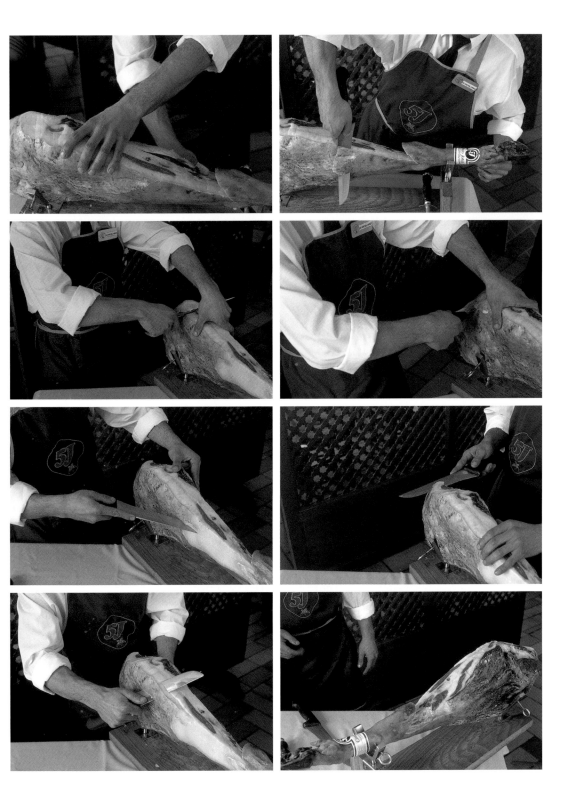

be kept straight until reaching the bone, when the ham is turned over to begin cutting on the flank, the broadest, most succulent part that offers the best possibilities for ample slices. Cutting should be done gently but firmly, following the lines of the muscle fibers. It must be kept in mind that the cutting gets more complicated the closer one gets to the bone. The rind, like the yellowish fat, must be eliminated as the cutting goes on to avoid its affecting the taste.

The first cut of the ham, called the sirloin or center, offers abundant fat content and is sweeter than the ham that is closer to the bone. The part that is most that is most protected by the skin, and also the most sinewy, is the "jarrete", sweet tasting and aromatic. On the other hand the saltiest part, very tasty and exquisite is the culata, where the nerves are concentrated.

In the case of a boneless ham (the most usual form of presentation for export, since it offers greater facility of handling and is more suitable for cutting by machine), skin and fat must be removed and the piece must be divided up before putting into the cutting machine. These hams can be cut lengthwise, from the knuckle to the tip or vice versa. Slices, as when cut by hand, should be very thin. And as in manual cutting, the part left open should be covered, in this case with a plastic, anti-grease covering, and kept at a temperature between 35° and 50° F.

Since exposure to oxygen alters the taste of the ham, whether cut by hand or by machine, it is essential to wait until the very last minute, since as soon as the meat is in contact with the air the ham begins to lose the delicious and evocative perfumes that characterize it.

To make sure that the slices of ham do not lose their characteristic aroma and taste, the ham should not be cut until the last minute, since exposure to air has a noticeably adverse affect on the flavor.

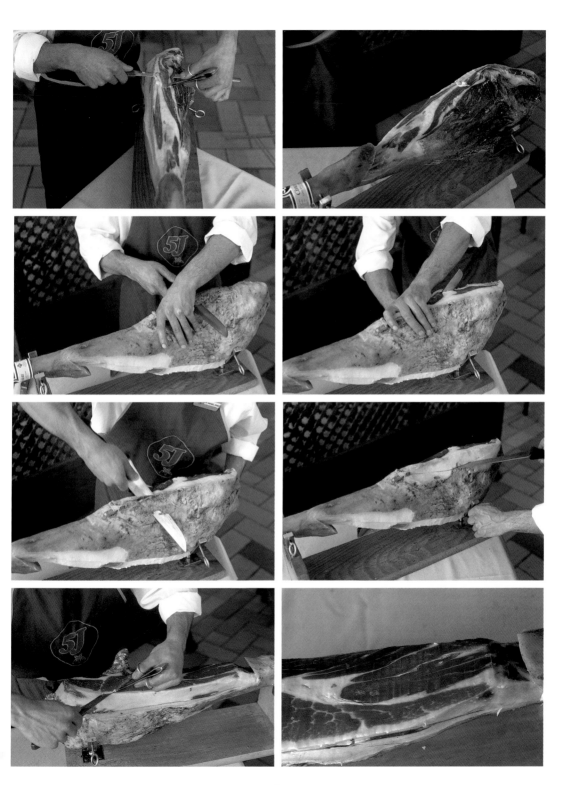

Cooking
with Ham

Cooking with Ham

Ham is one of the basic elements of Mediterranean cuisine, which is one of the healthiest, most nutritious and tastiest in the world.

This product, with all its widely known qualities, makes an excellent contribution to any menu. Ham is not reserved just for special occasions or luxurious tables, and the proof is that it forms a part of all sorts of dishes, many of them very easy to prepare, giving them a beautiful appearance and even better taste.

Without doubt, cured ham inspires an entire philosophy in the creation of recipes, providing color, "aroma" and, most of all, all the flavor that is needed. It plays a leading role in intuitive and imaginative cooking, but also in traditional gastronomy based on natural elements and products. Its possibilities are infinite and its presence more than justifiable, since it can appear in appetizers, main dishes and even desserts. It goes well with all sorts of vegetables, with lentils, beans, peas, lima beans, pastas, rice, and eggs and can be seasoned with parsley, rosemary, and pepper, but it also makes for excellent combinations with fruit like melons, figs, mangos or pineapples, providing contrasts of flavor that are really unbeatable. When using it with other products it is important not to make the mistake of disguising flavors, since the presence of the ham should help to enhance the combination. Foods that are incompatible with ham are butter, cream and fish, though sometimes attempts are made to use it in conjunction with seafood, such as scallops or cockles.

On these pages some dishes that can be made with this magnificent delicacy are suggested. They are recipes by chefs of established prestige that open the door to imagination and to the challenge of inventing new menus. But it is important not to forget that they are suggestions, and that there are vast possibilities for experiment in the kitchen. Good appetite!

Ham is one of the basic elements of the finest cuisine. Its particular characteristics make it possible for it to form a part of many exquisite dishes, both as the main ingredient or as a suggestive touch of flavor, that will fill any recipe with taste and color.

3

The culinary possibilities of ham are
infinite. Its qualities offer plenty of
reasons for its use in anything from
appetizers to desserts. The result will
always be a succulent dish rich in
flavor and "aroma".

6

5

7

9

Ham plays a leading role in cuisine
that is intuitive, full of imagination,
inspiration and ingenuity, highly
esthetic in appearance and with full-
bodied flavors and exquisite "aromas".

1. Bonito loin with "panceta" of Jabugo in civet.
   Xavier Sagristà, Restaurante Mas Pau.
2. Macaroni au gratin with truffles and Jabugo ham.
   Xavier Sagristà, Restaurante Mas Pau.
3. Stuffed scallions with perfume of truffles and Jabugo.
   Xavier Sagristà, Restaurante Mas Pau.
4. Cuban rice with quail's eggs and Jabugo salted meat.
   Xavier Sagristà, Restaurante Mas Pau.
5. Snail kebabs with artichokes and Jabugo.
   Xavier Sagristà, Restaurante Mas Pau.
6. Breaded young onions with trompetilla mushrooms and Jabugo ham.
   Xavier Sagristà, Restaurante Mas Pau.
7. Sirloin of Iberian pork with "panceta" of Jabugo in orange and garlic sauce.
   Xavier Sagristà, Restaurante Mas Pau.
8. Scallions with Jabugo vinaigrette.
   Xavier Sagristà, Restaurante Mas Pau.
9. Chard with raisin bread and "panceta" of Jabugo.
   Xavier Sagristà, Restaurante Mas Pau.
10. Cold thyme consommé with poached quail's egg and Jabugo ham.
    Xavier Sagristà, Restaurante Mas Pau.
11. Rabbit loin with olives and salted meat from Jabugo.
    Xavier Sagristà, Restaurante Mas Pau.
12. Texture salad with Jabugo fat.
    Carme Ruscalleda, Restaurante Sant Pau.
13. Risotto of rolled squid and Jabugo.
    Sergi Arola, Restaurante La Broche.
14. Vegetable and Jabugo grill.
    Ferran Adrià, Restaurante Bulli.
16. Seafood appetizer.
    Ferran Adrià, Restaurante Bulli.

14

15

Others titles by the publishing company

La Fundición, 15 Polígono Industrial Santa Ana 28529 Rivas-Vaciamadrid Madrid Tel. 34 91 666 50 01 Fax 34 91 301 26 83
asppan@asppan.com www.onlybook.com

Gaudí. Obra completa/
Gaudí. Complete works
ISBN (E): 84-89439-90-7
ISBN (GB): 84-89439-91-5

Barcelona, cuéntanos de Gaudí
Barcelona, tell us about Gaudí
Barcelona explican's Gaudí
ISBN (E): 84-89439-28-1
ISBN (GB): 84-89439-29-X
ISBN (C): 84-89439-35-X

Madrid
ISBN (E): 84-89439-88-5
ISBN (GB): 84-89439-89-3

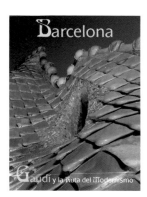

Barcelona, Gaudí y la ruta del
Modernismo/Barcelona, Gaudí and
Modernism
ISBN: (E)   84-89439-50-8
ISBN: (GB) 84-89439-51-6
ISBN: (D)   84-89439-58-3
ISBN: (IT)   84-89439-59-1
ISBN: (JP)   84-89439-60-5

Barcelona y Gaudí. Ejemplos
modernistas/Barcelona and Gaudí.
Examples of Modernist architecture
ISBN: (E)   84-89439-64-8
ISBN: (GB) 84-89439-65-6

Gaudí y el Modernismo en
Barcelona/Gaudí and Modernism in
Barcelona
ISBN: (E)   84-89439-50-8
ISBN: (GB) 84-89439-51-6